MARY

The Transparency
of God

M A R Y

The Transparency
of God

Chiara Lubich

New City Press
New York London Manila

Published in the United States by New City Press
202 Cardinal Rd., Hyde Park, NY 12538
www.newcitypress.com
©2003 New City Press

Translated by Eugene Selzer, Thomas Michael Hartmann
and Jerry Hearne (with revisions by Callan Slipper and Tom
Hartmann, Sr.) from the original Italian *Maria, Trasparenza di Dio*
©2003 Città Nuova, Rome, Italy

Cover picture by Yvonne Melançon
Cover design by Nick Cianfarani

Library of Congress Cataloging-in-Publication Data:
A catalog record for this book is available
from the Library of Congress.

ISBN 1-56548-192-5

Printed in the United States of America

Contents

Preface

It is a joy for me to preface this book of Chiara Lubich with a few words of greeting and recognition. Mary is inseparably linked to the Focolare Movement. Mary's "house of Nazareth" at Loreto could be called the cradle of this great new awakening in the Church. Where else could be its home, the hearth ("focolare" in Italian) where the Movement's love of Christ was kindled, if not the place in which Mary's yes lit up this fire upon the earth?

The deep love for Mary which has characterized Chiara's path from the very beginning is objectively based. These objective bases are rooted in the mystery of God and of Christ. I should like to highlight three of them.

1. There are moments in life when everything depends on saying: "Yes, right now!" In the history of humanity, too, there was a precise moment when everything was placed in the hands of a single person. It was the hour of the Annunciation. At that moment when the angel brought Mary the message, "Behold, you will conceive in your womb and bear a son, and you shall name him Jesus" (Lk 1:31), everything truly depended on her cooperation, on her "yes" or "no." Mary said "yes," and she lived that "yes" every day of her life. She lived it throughout the many hours, days, and years of her own path of faith.

2. The *Catechism of the Catholic Church* puts it this way: "What the Catholic faith believes about Mary is based on what it believes about Christ, and what it teaches about Mary illumines in turn its faith in Christ" (487). The role of Mary is completely derived from the role of Christ. And since he is the Messiah of Israel, the Son of God, she is truly "Mother of God." Consequently, the veneration of Mary is inseparable from the worship of Christ; in fact, true Marian piety leads irrevocably to Christ.

3. The veneration of Mary always includes the imitation of Mary, and this means also the way in which she took on responsibility. When Mary at Cana said to Jesus, "They have no wine" (Jn 2:3), she demonstrated an exquisite sensitivity for human needs. She showed that the criterion for genuine human piety is our readiness to imitate her in being attentive to the needs of our neighbor. Not only does love for Mary not distance us from one another, it draws us closer together.

It is my hope that these pages of Chiara, so rich in witness to Mary and in meditations about her, may nourish us and help very many people to say — like Mary and with her — their own "Here I am," their own "yes" to the plan and path that God has prepared for the life of each person. The multitude of people who have walked with Chiara along this path can testify that it leads — also by way of the experience of the cross — to happiness.

Vienna, Feast of St. Joseph
March 19, 2003

> + Cardinal Christoph Schönborn
> Archbishop of Vienna

This marvelous shade that contains the sun,
losing and finding itself therein:
it was Mary

Chiara Lubich

1.

Mary, the Transparency of God[1]

Among the many words
pronounced by the Father
in all of his Creation,
one was unique.

Not so much an object of thought
but more of intuition,
not so much the splendor of divine sun
but a cool and gentle shade,
like a little cloud, fresh and white,
that screens and adjusts the sun's rays
so that human eyes can see.

It was in the plans of Providence
that the Word be made flesh,
that a word, the Word, be written

---

1. This hymn to Mary was composed in the summer of 1959 in Fiera di
Primiero in the Dolomite Mountains of Italy where the author was
on vacation with members of the Focolare Movement; so many
people stopped by and became so united by the bonds of charity that
they gave birth to a temporary town, as they had done in previous
years. The little town was called "Mariapolis," that is, City of Mary.
Ed.

on earth in flesh and blood;
and this Word needed a background.

The heavenly harmonies
longed, out of love for us,
to transfer their peerless concert
within our tents;
and for this they needed a silence.

The Protagonist of all humanity,
who gave meaning to centuries past,
enlightened and drew after him centuries to come,
had to appear on this world's stage,
but needed a backdrop of white
to make him alone stand out.

The greatest design
that God-Love could invent
had to be drawn majestic
and divine, with all the colors
of virtue, and had to be found
in a heart composed and ready
to serve him.

This marvelous shade
that contains the sun,
losing and finding itself therein;
this white background
so immense, almost an abyss
that contains the Word which is Christ
submerging itself in him,
light in the Light;

this lofty silence
is silent no more,
for within it sing
the divine harmonies of the Word
and in him it becomes the note of notes,
almost setting the tone
for heaven's endless song;
this scene majestic and fair as nature,
synthesis of the beauty the Creator
lavished throughout the universe,
a little universe for the Son of God,
which is seen no more
because it yields its interests and its parts
to the One who was to come, and has come,
for what he had to do, and did;
this rainbow of virtue
that says "peace" to the entire world
because Peace it has given the world;
this creature, first thought of
in the mysterious abyss of the Trinity
and given to us,
was Mary.

Of her we do not speak,
of her we sing.
Of her we do not think,
but we call upon her and love her.
She is not the subject of study,
but of poetry.
The greatest geniuses of the world
have put brush and pen
at her service.

If Jesus incarnates the Word,
the Logos,
the Light,
Reason,
Mary personifies Art,
Beauty,
Love.

Masterpiece of the Creator,
Mary,
on whom the Holy Spirit
delighted to bestow all he invented,
and poured out so many of his inspirations.
Beautiful Mary!
About her we can never say enough.

2.

Mary in the Experience of the Focolare Movement[1]

I would like to present one of the cardinal points of our spirituality here, although she is so much more than just a point. I will, however, not set out to speak of Mary as perhaps one should when speaking of the world's most exalted being, since only the Church itself is capable of doing such a vast and demanding task. Instead, in the spirit of our Movement, I intend to discuss what we have understood about her, all the richness to be found in her as it has emerged in our experience and the outline of the light that her life has imprinted in our life. The subject of my talk, therefore, is "Mary in the Experience of the Focolare Movement."

---

1. What follows is a talk given by Chiara Lubich to a group of bishops, friends of the Focolare Movement, who had gathered at the Mariapolis Center in Castel Gandolfo, near Rome, on 16 February 1987. She has revised and expanded it for this present publication. *Ed.* Unless otherwise noted, all English translations are our own. *Trans.*

A New Vision

It seems to me that the present times call for a reintroduction of Mary. There are very many reasons for this, such as recent theological and ecumenical considerations. But also the invasion of a range of trends, including those of a secular, naturalistic, and hedonistic nature, sharply opposed to the transcendent, untarnished reality of Mary, has caused any authentic vision of her to be clouded, neglected, and overlooked.

Overall, the spirit of the Focolare implies rediscovering the everlasting truths of our faith. In the same way, we cherish the hope that the particular understanding God has given us of Mary may touch the mentality of people today to make them reconsider this person who is a "great sign" (Rv 12:1), God's true masterpiece.

In addition, it seems to us that Marian devotion needs to be revived, given that its most popular expressions (processions, novenas, Marian images, etc.) no longer have the appeal they once did. In order to love Mary as she deserves, I think we need to delve deeper, to understand more fully, a little better who she is.

To do this, we hope here to promote a new vision of Mary, one that is largely unknown, based on what God chose to show us about her.

Early Insights

Mary has been a part of our lives ever since the beginnings of the Focolare Movement, even before it officially existed. My earliest awareness of what was about to be born reaches way back to 1939 in Loreto, Italy, at the Madonna's house there. There I realized that the Lord was creating a new lifestyle — we called this the "fourth way" — for what would be a new spiritual family in the Church: the focolare community.[2] I had the intuition that a company of virgins would follow this path. So yes, Mary has been with us, ever since Loreto, silently waiting for all those who would follow her in her Movement.

Before we began to understand, through the charism given us by the Spirit, something new about the truths of our faith concerning Mary, the mother of Jesus generally meant devotion, charming affection, the possibility of having protection, and the Virgin to honor during the month of May. She was someone to call upon, a powerful subject that has continued to fascinate all kinds of artists in every age.

Later the newborn spirituality, which was gradually taking shape, deepened our previous, limited idea of Mary. It was as if she had been a beautiful, pure, and living statue that made our Christian expe-

---

2. This new calling is known as the "fourth way" because it brings together in an original manner the beauty of the three traditional paths that were previously known in the Church: family life, a celibate life in the world, and religious life. The focolare community, inspired by the family of Nazareth, exists in the midst of the world and is composed of virgins and married people who have consecrated their lives to God, albeit in different ways. *Ed.*

rience more beautiful and more sweet. But this was transformed and we were given a way of seeing her that more accurately reflects what lies in God's heart.

When the Focolare Movement began in Trent during the war (1939–45), I remember becoming aware personally of Mary in a rather new way. We were caught under a terrible air raid, which could easily have been the end for us. The shelter where we were hiding suddenly filled with dust. Completely covered, I got up from the ground, almost miraculously saved. Amid people's screams, I told my friends, "Just now, when we were in danger, I experienced a sharp stab in my soul — the pain of not being able to recite the Hail Mary here on earth anymore."

At the time, I could not grasp the meaning of those words and that suffering. Perhaps I was subconsciously expressing the feeling that, since we had survived, we would be able through the grace of God to give glory to Mary through the Work of Mary,[3] which was about to begin. Several decades later, it seems to me that that Hail Mary could have had the following meaning:

---

3. The Focolare Movement was approved by the Roman Catholic Church under the name *Work of Mary*. Article 2 of its General Statutes reads: "The Work of Mary bears this name because its typical spirituality, its ecclesial features, the variety of its members, its universal extension, its relationship of collaboration and friendship with Christians of different churches and ecclesial communities, with people of different faiths, and with people of goodwill, and the fact that its president is a lay person and a woman, all show its special bond with Mary most holy, mother of Christ and of every person. The Work of Mary wishes — as far as possible — to be a presence of Mary, almost a continuation of Mary on earth." See also below, pp. 31, 36-37. *Ed.*

Hail Mary, full of grace. Be happy Mary, because new and abundant graces are about to come down to the earth in this twentieth century.

The Lord is with you. The Lord is at work to honor you in a new way.

Blessed are you among women. New blessings are about to be brought to you by your children and by many Christians and other people who until now have not cared to or were not able to get to know you.

Blessed is the fruit of your womb, Jesus. Wherever in the world that you are present through the Work of Mary, your son will flourish again in the midst of you.

Holy Mary, Mother of God, pray for us sinners. Sinners, but chosen in this moment to be empty chalices to contain your new presence on earth.

Now . . . In the present moment, that extremely precious moment in which you, as our mother and teacher, instruct us how to live.

. . . and at the hour of our death. Death, which in the fury of war you fixed in our hearts and in the hearts of those who followed us, as the mainspring to throw ourselves into a new life, the true life.

Amen. Let it be so for the centuries to come, as it has been until now, and much, much more so.

In the years that followed, Mary stood guard over the first focolare house. Each day when we woke, we would pray "because you are forsaken" to Jesus. This expressed the driving force behind our new life. We would conclude by saying "because you are desolate" to Mary, even though we did not yet understand the profound mystery that these words contain.

References were made to Mary, especially as the Immaculate One, when the original group of Focolarini and I, emerging from the rest of the community, followed our special calling, and formed what was then called the *schiera bianca* (the white company). The words of our total consecration to God were formulated so that it was given through Mary's maternal heart; after all, she was the woman who had given herself to God as a virgin contrary to the customs of her time.

Here I must mention a letter that I wrote to my friends in 1946, which reads:

The Feast of the Immaculate Conception,
Queen of Virgins

My dearest sisters, most beloved among all,

To all of you who are so far away, although a single ideal of unity and virginity links you to me, I send greetings from the "white company," which met for the first time today, in secret, to begin nurturing our souls for a life of virginity!

We all placed ourselves (there are forty of us) in Mary's immaculate heart, signing our names behind a painting of the Madonna that hangs in our hall. (I signed for all of you who are far away, yet so present among us.)

Three years ago, I was alone when I consecrated my life to God, which I gave to him through the hands of Mary Immaculate.

Now there are forty of us!

This white company of souls, like towers of ivory, must support the structure of the entire Ideal.[4]

Virginity, or death!

There is a fortress to bring down: the world, the devil, sin! It is practically invincible.

Only lilies can conquer such strongholds!

Coming together for a couple of hours on this sunny morning of the feast Mary Immaculate, we placed ourselves under the special protection of Saint Agnes, virgin and martyr, and Saint Ambrose, the patron saint of virginity.

We want to imitate Saint Agnes by giving our young lives completely by the powerful strength of our purity which shouts in its immaculate splendor, *Unus est dilectus meus!* (my love is but one).

If a saint says that only a company of virgins in every city can save the world, *we must be that company!*

We have read some of the marvelous writings of Saint Ambrose on virginity. May your guardian angels tell you something of that divine inspiration which entered our hearts. When that saint lived — he was enchanted with virginity — mothers used to lock young girls inside in order to

---

4. Ever since the early years of World War II, Chiara gave the name "Ideal" to the light she felt shine within her, which seemed to come from above. Thus the term refers to all the ideas that led to the founding and life of the Focolare Movement — both its spirituality and organization. *Ed.*

keep them from running to listen to him and follow the way of virginity. We too, kept by the sweet voice of a mother, the immaculate Virgin, have sworn faithfulness to the Spouse of virgins in order to work for the coming of God's kingdom on earth.

Greetings from everyone.

Look up, beyond the stars and the angels, to the heart of God. From there virginity descended to earth, an eminent virtue that exceeds nature and makes angels out of people.

And like angels, you too walk toward Heaven.

In the Immaculate Heart of Mary,
Chiara

Then, to tell the truth, we did not speak much about Mary for a number of years. Each day the Eucharist — bond of unity — nourished us. God, in the meantime, was etching those "new" truths (although they are ancient, too) on each of our souls in fiery letters. They took up all of our minds, hearts, and strength, and we translated them into life. God is Love, the Will of God, the New Commandment, Jesus Forsaken, the Word of Life, Unity, and Jesus in the Midst[5] were the truths that became fundamental points for the new-sprung spirituality, which was both personal and collective. Our goal was to experience Jesus among us ever more often and ever more fully.

_____

5. "For where two or three are gathered together in my name, there am I in the midst of them" (Mt 18:20).

22

When in 1947 someone asked why we never spoke of Mary, we answered that she was a gate that leads to God. "Hail, O Gate of the Sublime Mystery," sounds the Akathistos hymn.[6] A gate is not a gate unless it opens and allows free passage. A door that is always closed is really a wall. Those who stop at the gate do not reach God. The gate is for Jesus.

The Virgin is the one who is empty of self, utterly self-forgetful. She is the created being who knows that she is created, even when filled with God.

She was using the same method for our Movement that she had used for the Church: keeping herself in the shadows in order to highlight her Son, who is God.

Magnificent Light

Precisely because Jesus was in our midst, we began to understand something about Mary that we previously had not been aware of. He began to show her to us from his point of view. As a result, in a manner of speaking, Mary had her "official" debut in our Movement. Jesus unveiled her as great, with greatness in proportion to how much she had managed to disappear. When this happened in 1949, the year was filled with special graces. It was an enlightened period in our history.

6. "Inno Acatisto," in *Lodi alla Madonna* (Rome, 1980), p. 48.

Word of God

We then understood that, like a precious stone, Mary is a rare and unique person set within the Holy Trinity. She is totally made up of the Word of God; it enfolds her entirely (see Lk 2:19, 51). And if the Word is the splendor of the Father, then Mary, completely shaped by the Word, is incomparably beautiful.

We were so deeply moved by these realizations that even now we cannot forget them. It still seems to us, as it did at the time, that only angels could stammer something about her.

The Magnificat (Lk 1:46–55) also displays how Mary is completely the Word of God. The originality of this prayer lies in the fact that it is a collection of sentences quoted from the scriptures. This makes us understand that the scriptures had nourished Mary so much that she was in the habit of quoting them to express herself.

R. Laurentin writes: "In the Magnificat, each part of every sentence echoes a passage from the Bible. . . . Mary is so permeated with the Word of God that she is its echo. We should not, therefore, be surprised when God answers her in the same way. At the Annunciation, the divine messenger speaks in the language of the scriptures to the Virgin, who had been continually nourished by them."[7]

"The ark held the Law," writes Saint Maximus of Turin, "and Mary carried the gospel. . . . While the

---

7. R. Laurentin, *La Vergine Maria* (Rome, 1984), p. 33.

ark emitted the voice of God, Mary carried the Word inside, the Word made flesh."[8]

Although she was uniquely perfect, Mary's particular characteristic was the vocation of every Christian: to repeat Christ, the truth, the Word, each according to the personality given by God. We Christians, as indeed all the rest of humanity, are all as equal as the leaves of a tree, yet each of us is completely different. Each one, in fact, sums up in himself or herself the whole of creation. Therefore since each one of us is "a creation" in ourselves, we are equal to others and, at the same time, different from them.

Seeing Mary as essentially God's word seems to us to be charged with meaning, especially for dialogue. If Mary may be a stumbling block to full unity with our sisters and brothers of evangelical churches, what will happen when they, who underline the value of scripture so powerfully, discover she is the personification of those very scriptures?

Mother of God

The figure of Mary has attracted us ever since our souls began to contemplate her. A new love for her began. She responded to this love evangelically by revealing herself more clearly to our souls in her most exalted form: Mother of God, Theotokos.

Just the tiniest intuition of this mystery was enough to render us speechless in adoration and in

---

8. Maximus of Turin, "Sermo XLII" in *Patrologia Latina* 57, pp. 738–40.

thanksgiving toward God for having accomplished so much in one of his creations.

Mary was not just that young girl from Nazareth, as we had previously thought, or the most beautiful of God's creations, or even the heart that contains and surpasses the love of all the world's mothers. She was the Mother of God.

She loomed larger in our eyes than ever. We had been totally unaware, and it was as if we were getting to know her for the first time.

In the past, we had seen Mary in relationship to Christ and the saints — to make a comparison — as in the heavens where there is the moon (Mary) in relationship to the sun (Christ) and the stars (the saints). Now, it was no longer so. The Mother of God embraced, like a vast, blue sky, the sun itself, God himself.

Mary, in fact, is the Mother of God because she is the mother of the humanity of the one person of the Word, who is God and who wished to become man. The Word, however, can never be thought separate from the Father or the Holy Spirit. Jesus himself, the son of Mary, tells Philip when the apostle asks him to show them the Father: "Whoever has seen me has seen the Father. . . . I am in the Father and the Father is in me" (Jn 14:9–11).

We had contemplated Mary as being set within the Trinity, but now, because of her Son, in her own particular way, we saw her as containing the Trinity.

Maximus the Confessor, a Father of the Church, writes: "Indeed, through his incarnation, the Word of God demonstrates theology by the very fact that he displays in himself the Father and the Holy Spirit.[9] The Father in his entirety and the Holy Spirit in his entirety were essentially and perfectly within the Son in his entirety, even when he became incarnate, and even though they did not themselves become incarnate."[10]

Full of adoration, we admired God who, in limitless love for this privileged created being, in a sense made himself "little" before her.[11] According to Paul, Jesus, who is God, "emptied himself" (Phil 2:7). And all this began in Mary's womb.

When we began to comprehend Mary's greatness, our souls wanted to shout out, "Only now do we know Mary!"

Contemplating Mary as the Mother of God and the fact that God gave her the ability, in a way, to contain the Trinity, Louis de Montfort wrote: "In that same paradise, Mary is the paradise of God, and into her ineffable world the Son of God came to work miracles, to guard it and find there his own delight. God made our world for 'man the traveler'; he made another, paradise, for 'man the blessed'; but he made another for himself and gave it the name Mary."[12]

---

9. In this instance, "theology" refers to the intimate life of the Trinity as it is manifested in the economy of salvation, that is, in how the divine Persons relate to human beings.

10. Maximus the Confessor, "Oratio dominica," in *Patrologia Greca* 90, p. 876.

11. In his *Hymn to the Nativity*, Saint Ephraem the Syrian writes, "He who was equal to his Father from all eternity became a child in Mary's womb; he gave us his greatness and took on our smallness" (*Corpus Scriptorum Cristianorum Orientalium* 187, p. 180).

12. Louis Marie Grignon de Montfort, *Il segreto di Maria* (Rome: Centro Mariano Monfortano, 1972), p. 19.

Peter Chrysologus adds: "Only Mary contains him whom the world can never contain. Only Mary carries in her arms the One who carries the world. And only Mary generated her creator and nourished the One who nourishes the living."[13]

If Mary is the Word of God lived out, she heads the entire array of Christ's disciples and is the first disciple. And she is in no way an "obstacle" to our relationship with Christ.

If Mary personifies the Word of God, the Christian is right in venerating her and following her as a leader after Christ. For this reason she is the subject of song and of painting, poetry pays her homage, monuments are erected to her, and processions honor her on feast days dedicated to her.

Moreover, if Mary is the Mother of God, she is very different from any other Christian. So much so that God adorned her with such beauty that he delighted in her and exalted her, as the angel's words proclaim: "Hail, favored one! The Lord is with you" (Lk 1:28). A special place at God's side awaits her.

It is easy to understand, therefore, why images of Mary appear in Catholic and Orthodox churches. Every expression of honor and affection toward her becomes meaningful.

---

13. Peter Chrysologus, "Sermo 143," in *Patrologia Latina* 52, p. 583.

Our Model

A further understanding we had of Mary during the period of light which took place in the summer of 1949 was of Mary's "exemplary" nature, of how she is our "prototype," as Pope Paul VI later defined her.[14] Mary is our model. She is that which we "should be"; while we saw that each one of us was that which "could be" Mary.

That summer, the Lord had chosen a number of women Focolarine, two or three men Focolarini, and a married Focolarino to receive special gifts of light. One day, when we were already fused into a single soul by the love of God, which enfolded us in a special way, we felt a powerful impulse to consecrate ourselves to Mary. We asked Jesus in the Eucharist, to give us to his mother as only he knew how.[15]

What happened was something extraordinary. This was more than merely an act of devotion, without any real content. Something truly took

---

14. See also Paul VI, "Omelia nella festività dell Assunta," 15 August 1966, in *Insegnamenti di Paolo VI* 4 (1966) (Vatican City: Poliglotta Vaticana, 1967), p. 1065; *Lumen Gentium* 63–65 (in *Enchiridion Vaticanum* 1:439–41).

15. "The consecration described here," explains the theologian Marisa Cerini, "reflects the original consecrations to God that can be found in the Bible, whether they were collective (such as that of the chosen people) or personal. God always initiated them: it was God who called people to dedicate themselves to him and who 'consecrated' those who responded to his invitation; it was he who made them sacred or holy as he is holy, giving his own sanctity. In a similar fashion, the group's consecration to Mary, entrusted to Jesus in the Eucharist so he might bring it about, is God's work. The result is that they are clothed in Mary's purity." *Ed.*

place. In that consecration, it seemed to us that Mary clothed us in her "immaculateness."

And we realized that the prayer to Mary composed later by Paul VI, "teach us . . . to be as immaculate as you are"[16] — could come true for us.

We dared to hope that what Louis de Montfort had written about certain people who dedicate themselves to Mary could happen to us as a group. "The main result is that Mary comes to live in the soul, to the point that it is no longer just the soul that lives but Mary who lives in it. She becomes, in a manner of speaking, the very soul of that soul."[17]

God's plan for our group, and consequently for the newborn community, was in a sense, we realized, to relive Mary.

We also saw each of us as a tiny Mary, similar to her, as a daughter who has *solely* the features of her mother. I remember it was then that I looked upon our mother, Mary, for the first time with the gaze of a daughter. But now it was as a daughter who saw her

---

16. Paul VI, "Il patrocinio di Maria sulla Pentecoste perenne," 25 October 1969, at the Basilica of Saint Mary Major, in *Insegnamenti di Paolo VI* 7 (1969) (Vatican City: Poliglotta Vaticana, 1970), p. 687. With regard to sharing Mary's purity, Maximilian Kolbe writes: "Let's completely devote ourselves to her, with no limitations, in order to be her servants, her children, her things, and her property in such an unconditional way that we will be mystically transformed into her living, speaking, and working in this world. She is the Immaculate Conception, and she remains so in us and transforms us into herself by making us immaculate" (*Gli scritti di Massimiliano Kolbe: eroe di Oswiecim e beato della Chiesa* 1 [Florence, 1975], p. 896).

17. Louis Grignon de Montfort, "Il segreto di Maria," no. 55, in *Trattato della vera devozione alla santa Vergine e il segreto di Maria* (Rome, 1985), p. 205.

real self in her mother. And intuitively I began to grasp what may have gone through Mary's heart as she saw herself in us. This thought moved me for quite a while.

We realized for the first time, in an unforgettable way, that Mary was our mother. The words of the young Thérèse of Lisieux came true for us. "I understood . . . that I was her daughter, and so I could only call her 'mother.' "[18]

Indeed there and then the conviction was so strong that our natural mothers seemed distant, and they became almost like any other woman in the world. Mary had taken her rightful place. She was, as John the Geometer writes, "mother of each and every one of us and more mother than our own mothers."[19]

Regarding Mary as our true mother, Louis de Montfort writes: "Just as in natural childbearing . . . there is a father and a mother, in the spiritual realm . . . there is a father who is God and a mother who is Mary. All true children of God . . . have God as father and Mary as mother and those who do not have Mary as mother do not have God as father."[20]

The theologian J. H. Nicolas seems to have some affinity with our experience, since his writings contain similar elements: "What Mary's action would bring is a kind of perfection to nature and

18. See also Thérèse of Lisieux, "Ms A, 56v-57r," in *Opere complete* (Rome, 1997), p. 166.
19. Giovanni il Geometra, "Discorso sull'Assunzione," no. 66, in A. Wenger, *L'Assomption de la T. S. Vierge dans la Tradition Byzantine du V° au X° siècle* (Paris, 1955), pp. 410–12.
20. Louis Grignon de Montfort, *Trattato della vera devozione a Maria* (Rome, 2000), p. 50.

creation, which is made capable of overcoming hesitation and of opening up to its Creator and Savior, of returning to something of its *first innocence*, a tranquility, and even heals the 'reflexes' of pride and rebellion. Everything that she received through pure grace, Mary obtains for us and bequeaths on us. Through her, we can be reborn. She is — actively and gently, humanly and divinely — our mother."[21]

Since we understood that together we were truly called to be like Mary, we also gradually realized that we had to live God's Word. We had to be God's Word and nothing else. In particular we had to live Jesus forsaken, who is the Word fully revealed.[22]

We had to safeguard God's Word within. By becoming holy through the Word, each of us generated Jesus in ourselves for ourselves and for those around us. Like this it would have been possible to say that, in a way, the words "blessed is the fruit of thy womb, Jesus" applied to us.

"If someone, through their word," writes Gregory the Great, "inspires love for the Lord to be born in the soul of a neighbor, they practically generate the Lord . . . and become the Lord's mother."[23]

---

21. J. H. Nicolas, *Theotókos: Le mystére de Marie* (Paris: Desclée, 1965), p. 183.
22. Jesus is the Word of the Father, the revelation that God is Love. In the abandonment that he experiences on the cross (see Mt 27:46; Mk 15:34), he reaches the depths of humanity's sin and distance from God. By doing this, he proves just how far God's love extends. *Ed.*
23. Gregory the Great, quoted by Saint Bede the Venerable in *Commento al Vangelo di Marco*, vol. 1 (Rome, 1970), pp. 116–17; see also *Lumen Gentium* 65.

In our consecration to Mary, it seemed to us that Jesus repeated what he had done with John the Apostle and Mary — he gave us to her to be her children. "Woman, behold, your son" (Jn 19:26). He also helped us do what every Christian should: imitate John at the foot of the cross when Jesus invited him to take Mary to be with him. "Behold, your mother" (Jn 19:27).

According to Vatican II, Christians should be forged by the Holy Spirit and Mary. "The text [*Lumen Gentium* 65] suggests that whenever Christ is born in the hearts of the faithful, he is still 'conceived by the Holy Spirit and born from the Virgin.' "[24]

Christians are thus formed by the Holy Spirit and Mary. The goal, of course, is not to remain in Mary but to become another Jesus.

We understood this clearly in 1949. The day after our consecration to Mary, the Lord helped us realize during meditation that Christ was coming to dwell in us, fused into one, and in each of us individually. "In a way," Paul VI says of a Christian who lives God's Word, "the miracle of God's incarnation occurs inside us, just as it did for the Madonna."[25]

These were the first clarifications that the Holy Spirit made to us about Mary.

Now, many years later, we can see how these were forerunners of those graces and illuminations from

---

24. J. Galot, "Maria, tipo e modello della Chiesa," in G. Barauna, ed., *La Chiesa del Vaticano II* (Florence, 1965), p. 1169.
25. From a speech by Paul VI on August 15, 1970.

God that molded and built our Movement, which spontaneously took Mary's name.

At the time, the young Work of Mary was present in those few who had been privileged to take part in these spiritual intuitions. As it grew, in order to be united with others, those graces were shared as much as possible.

Further Illuminations

Then more light came.

Once, for example, we seemed to understand, by a special intuition, the meaning of Mary's title, Mother of Beautiful Love. We spontaneously wanted to repeat, "Ah, you are beautiful, my beloved, ah, you are beautiful" (Song 1:15).

Mary is mother of a love that is beautiful. She taught us who were united with her to grasp the "beautiful love" of God that exists beneath all creation. Everything seemed linked by this love. For example, we saw, looking outside of ourselves, that nature was animated by a spiritual sun as well as a natural one. We saw everything living out of love: a river flows to the sea out of love, water evaporates out of love, and rain falls out of love.

We saw how everything on earth is in a relationship of love with everything else: each with every other thing. This was a golden thread that connected all that is.

I felt I had been created to be a gift for those around me, and that God had created those around me as gifts for me. As in the Trinity, where the Father is completely given to the Son, and the Son is completely given to the Father, each person is completely given to the others.

We saw in Mary the whole creation purified and redeemed, and we understood how all creation returns to God through Mary.

She is the Mother of Beautiful Love.

And it seemed to us that she shared some of her maternity of love with us.

Today the Work of Mary is very developed.[26] We know how enriching its spiritual maternity has been for many, so it is obvious why in those first years the Madonna introduced us to our specific kind of outreach: a spiritual maternity embracing the widest variety of people in the Church and humanity in general.

One day, I remember, as we looked to Mary, we seemed to recognize how much she loved the Father. She had been taught by the Son to love the Father, and as a result the Father loved her even more. She seemed to be the fulfillment of Jesus' words to the Father, "you loved them even as you loved me" (Jn 17:23). The Father loved her *just as* he loved his own son.

---

26. On 10 July 1968, in a public audience at Saint Peter's Basilica, Paul VI defined the Focolare Movement as "a tree that is already very fertile and very rich." See Paul VI, *Al Movimento dei Focolari* (Rome: Città Nuova, 1979). *Ed.*

We saw her as the *daughter* par excellence, "the beloved daughter of the Father,"[27] as Vatican II referred to her.

She is God's daughter as, though in an utterly different way, Jesus is God's Son. For Jesus was the Son begotten through the Father's love, his "beloved Son" (Col 1:13), as Paul calls him. In a similar way, we spontaneously began to call her, who was God's daughter, the "woman of love." Truly, she was extraordinarily beautiful!

We can still remember appreciating Mary's beauty and, since we did not know anyone who equaled her, we asked her to form a family here on earth, made up of children who would be *wholly her* and share her same spiritual features.

Now we feel that Mary herself suggested that prayer to us. Although we are absolutely unworthy, she intended to take us and weave together what would eventually be the Work of Mary.

The call to live like Mary would repeat itself a number of times in our history.

Another day, for example — and this is a particularly meaningful episode — I entered a church. My heart was full of confidence, and I think the Holy Spirit inspired me and placed words in my mouth. I asked Jesus why he, who had remained in every corner of the world in his sweet Eucharist, had not found a way to also leave here his mother, whose help we needed so badly on the journey of life.

---

27. *Lumen Gentium* 53.

In the silence, Jesus seemed to answer me from the tabernacle: "I have not left her because I want to see her again in you. Even if you are not immaculate, my love will virginize you, and you, all of you, will open your arms and hearts as mothers of humanity, which, as in times past, thirsts for God and for his mother. It is you who now must soothe pains, soothe wounds, dry tears. Sing her litanies and strive to mirror yourself in them."[28]

It was a moment when God re-emphasized in our hearts the conviction that the Work of Mary had to be nothing other than a mystical presence of Mary.

At the time there were many challenges, including physical ones. I remember that it was only possible to go on living by never ceasing to look to Jesus forsaken, to the wound of his abandonment. Yet after my conversation with Jesus about Mary, I seemed to comprehend — with an understanding that comes from the Holy Spirit — that to be like Mary, to be another Mary, it was necessary to go decisively beyond the wounds, necessary to embrace the forsaken Jesus so that in us could shine the risen Jesus, the new person. Only in this way could we be like Mary.

Because of all these experiences, not only did our Movement take the name of Mary, but we gave her name to many of the things we do.

---

28. Chiara Lubich, *Meditations* (New City, London 1989), pp. 52-53; cf. also, *Christian Living Today: Meditations* (New York: New City Press, 1997), pp. 126–27.

Each time we come together, the members of the Work of Mary form a Mariapolis, a temporary "city of Mary." Our small towns are also called Mariapolises, and buildings used for spiritual development are known as Mariapolis Centers. Mariapolis is also the title of a number of publications of ours.

Mary Desolate

There is a side of Mary — a moment of her life — that has always intrigued us from the Movement's very beginnings. It is Mary at the foot of the cross in her desolation: Mary Desolate.

I would like to speak of her as only angels can. Yet when I think of her, words fail.

Something I could say — and this makes the whole subject less painful — is that if I am in the grace of God I am the fruit of Mary's desolation. This is true for all of us. My very being, our very being, lessens this immense pain by giving it a meaning of love.

We saw furthermore how the riches that Jesus bore in himself were fully displayed when he was crucified.[29] His abandonment completely revealed his nature as Savior. Jesus, in his forsakenness, gave himself totally. In his forsakenness, he reached the height of suffering and transformed it into love. And the result of this is the greatest glory for God because he offers God a new creation.

---

29. See also Chiara Lubich, *Jesus: The Heart of His Message: Unity and Jesus Forsaken* (New York: New City Press, 1985); and *The Cry: Jesus Crucified and Forsaken in the History and Life of the Focolare Movement* (New York: New City Press, 2001).

Like Jesus, Mary also had her moment of culmination. It was her desolation, which is her forsakenness.

Today scholars wonder to whom John's words in the Book of Revelation refer, when they present a mother in a cosmic vision, almost a synthesis of creation, with the sun, the moon and the stars. This woman is about to give birth to a son: "A great sign appeared in the sky, a woman clothed with the sun, with the moon under her feet and on her head a crown of twelve stars. She was with child and wailed aloud in pain as she labored to give birth" (Rv 12:1–2).

After having come to know about and having lived Mary's desolation in our Movement, and therefore after having been enlightened about her suffering, it is my opinion — I share it with many others — that the woman in Revelation is the desolate, yet glorious Mary, mother of the whole Church.

Given the mysterious relationship between Mary and the Church, since she is both daughter of the Church and mother of the Church, it seems to me that this expression could be used of both Mary and the Church.

There would be a lot to say on this subject, which to those of us who try to love Mary and the Church as much as we can, is so sweet and yet so beyond words. From this brief hint, however, we can intuitively sense the majesty of God's plan for Mary, who is desolate, yet glorious.

For the moment, however, let us return to the straightforward episode of Mary's desolation that the gospel narrates.

When Jesus points to John and tells Mary, "Woman, behold, your son" (Jn 19:26), those words probably sounded to Mary like a substitution. Mary experiences the spiritual trial of losing Jesus, not only because he is dying, but because someone else is taking his place.

Mary's acceptance of God's will on Calvary — her fiat — was quite different from her first fiat at the Annunciation. There she, who had consecrated herself to God as a virgin for her entire life, seemed to be asked to change her plans. And she was to become Jesus' mother while remaining a virgin.

Her second fiat, at the foot of the cross, meant letting go of Jesus. Only by doing this could she become mother of us all and take on the maternity of countless women and men.

Mary "offered [Jesus] at Golgotha to the Eternal Father and sacrificed her mother's rights and love. . . . She who was physically the mother of the head became the spiritual mother of the entire body," wrote Pius XII.[30]

Through her desolation, we have always thought that Mary fully accomplished God's plan for her. It was in an indescribable suffering that was love and, consequently, a gift of glory to the Father and the Son she was called to give. In this she became mother of the Church — not only mother of Jesus but of his Mystical Body as well.

---

30. Pius XII, *Mystici Corporis,* 29 July 1943, in *Acta Apostolicae Sedis* 35 (1943), pp. 247–48; see also *Lumen Gentium* 58 and note 11.

It is difficult to even imagine how much Mary suffered when Jesus cried out, "My God, my God, why have you forsaken me?" (Mt 27:46, Mk 15:34). She would have wanted to be closest to him then, yet she had given him away. She received no privileges for having been his mother. In the face of Jesus' demand that she should take on another kind of motherhood, she was allowed neither to grieve nor to be troubled.

In the moment of his forsakenness, therefore, Jesus had neither father nor mother. He was like a nothingness born of nothing.

Mary, too, was suspended in this void. Her greatness had been Jesus, her Son. Now she was forced to lose him. In her desolation Mary, because of God's will for her, seems to not share her Son's pain or his work of redemption. She appears separate from her Son while, alone, he offers his life for everyone, including her.

At the same time, however, she shared his suffering with unthinkable, one could almost say infinite, intensity. It was at that precise moment that she became mother of us all.

"This did not happen without a divine plan," writes Benedict XV. "Mary suffered so greatly and almost died with her dying son. She renounced her maternal rights for the sake of humanity's salvation and sacrificed her son to the point . . . that we can rightfully say that she redeemed the human race together with Christ."[31]

---

31. Benedict XV, *Inter Sodalicia,* 22 March 1918, in *Acta Apostloicae Sedis* 10 (1918), p. 182.

This gives us some insight into our potential greatness as human beings. Each of us is truly destined to be another Jesus, to be divine, in some way, as he is.

"Amen, amen, I say to you, unless a grain of wheat falls to the ground and dies, it remains just a grain of wheat; but if it dies, it produces much fruit," Jesus tells the Apostles before his Passion (Jn 12:24). If the Son of God died — Saint Paul calls him the "firstborn from the dead" (Col 1:18) — it was in order to give life to many children of God.

Mary also paid for us. And having given Jesus away, she should not receive in return people who are only partially Jesus but those who are *genuinely "another Jesus,"* with his light and with his love. Persons who are just like him: "You loved them even as you loved me" (Jn 17:23).

Origen was the first to call Mary "mother" in a way that was more than her simply being the mother of Jesus. "Mary," he wrote, "had no other son but Jesus, and Jesus said to his mother, 'Behold, your son,' not, 'Behold, I am your son.' It is as if to say, 'this other is also Jesus who you bore.' In fact, those who are perfect do not live for themselves but Christ lives in them. Since Christ lives in them, it is as if he says to Mary, 'Here is your son, Christ.'"[32]

In her desolation at having renounced her maternal rights, Mary suffered the spiritual trial of feeling just like any other ordinary woman, no longer bearing the title of what she truly was, Mother of

---

32. Origen, "Comm. In Johannem" 1:6, in *Patrologia Greca* 14:32.

God. Similarly, in his forsakenness, Jesus appeared to be an ordinary man, no longer God.

I think those who have received a special mission or calling from God can comprehend something of Mary's mysterious suffering. God often tests these people with a spiritual dark night, when they feel as if they have lost the light he had granted them, as to a prophet, for the good of his people. When this happens, these people, although they had been consistently aware of their calling, suffer indescribably and cry out at such abandonment.

This was the price, therefore, that Mary paid with Jesus for our birth.

It was here that she became Mother of the Church. It was here — we can perceive through intuition — that she also in some way earned her assumption to heaven with her glorified body. The law that loss becomes gain was at work here. She, who had been overshadowed by the Holy Spirit so that she gave birth to the God-Man, lost her divine maternity. As a result she could hope to gain bodily entrance into heaven through her Son himself.

"She who experienced the 'com-passion,'" writes the theologian Nicolas, "deserved the joy of the Resurrection and perhaps was more worthy of her Assumption."[33]

In his forsakenness, Jesus appeared to be only a man. In her desolation — her desolation is her

---

33. J. H. Nicolas, *Theotókos: Le Mystére de Marie*, p. 157.

forsakenness, since her son was God — Mary seemed to be a woman like any other.

There is, however, a difference between these parallel passions of Jesus and Mary. Jesus was alone; Mary was with a son, John.

In addition, from the way Jesus pronounced the words, "Woman, behold, your son" (Jn 19:26) and told the disciple, "Behold, your mother"(Jn 19:27), we can immediately see that this was not merely Jesus' filial love for his mother. Nor was it to safeguard John. No, these words have particular meaning and constitute another reality.

In this moment Mary was entrusted with the Church, which is represented by John, as her child. At the same time, in the person of John, the Church received Mary as its mother.

"It was precisely on Golgotha," John XXIII affirms, "that the Redeemer . . . as his highest testament, established that his mother would also be the mother of all the redeemed: *Ecce Mater tua*."[34]

And if we read the next sentence in the gospel, we find: "And from that hour the disciple took her into his home" (Jn 19:27). So the task of the Church and every Christian is to take Mary home, live with Mary, and go to Christ with and through Mary. She is our spiritual mother, a mother who nourishes Christians with salvation that is born from her womb, as Augustine said.[35]

---

34. John XXIII, "All'udienza generale" (9 September 1961) in *L'Osservatore Romano*, 10 September 1961.
35. See also Augustine, "Sermo 291" in *Patrologia Latina* 38:1319; and in *Lodi alla Madonna*, p. 67.

Jesus could have said to John on the cross, "John, I redeem you through my passion." Instead, in the moment that he redeemed us, Jesus gave us to Mary. And since he did this, there is no other way to take full advantage of this redemption than to do Jesus' will: take Mary home, and through her, reach Jesus. "And from that hour the disciple took her into his home" (Jn 19:27).

This thought can revolutionize the lives of many Christians.

We love Mary, we pray to her, and we have pictures of her in our homes. There are churches and monuments built in her honor. She is present in the Catholic Church, in other churches, and in the hearts of the faithful.

But we do not usually think it is our duty to take Mary into our homes and live with her as John did. So great a mother can feed our undernourished Christianity and enlighten us with her advice. We could live in the presence of she who is so much the highest perfection of motherhood that many people, especially the elderly, call out to her from their deathbeds.

By the grace of God, throughout our history the members of the Work of Mary have always sought to take her into their homes and keep her always in mind, especially as Mary Desolate.

This is something of how in the Focolare people think of Mary and love her.

Especially as Mary Desolate, her example helps them resolve the trials of life, from the simpler ones, in those who are just beginning their spiritual paths, to the more complex ones, in those who are more advanced.

The ways in which members of the Focolare imitate Mary Desolate will be dealt with later.[36]

We will also be able to make clear how, by living Mary Desolate, we have come to understand what the Movement calls the *Via Mariae*, the Way of Mary, in which various stages of the Madonna's life represent steps that a member of the Movement has to follow in climbing to perfection.

Nothing But the Gospel

Thinking of how Mary expresses the whole of the gospel, I thought I would conclude by confiding a personal experience.

Independently of all these considerations on Mary, which obviously mean a lot to me, I notice there is one thought that keeps coming back to my soul: Leave only the gospel to those who follow you. If you do this, the Ideal will remain.[37] It is obvious that in the age you and the others live in, there have been ideas, phrases, and slogans that have served to make the gospel relevant. But these thoughts, these sayings, these almost "words of life" will pass away.

When unity between Christians has practically been achieved, ecumenism will no longer be a far-off goal. When some kind of world unity has been estab-

36. See pp. 49–68.
37. See p. 21, note 4.

lished, there will be no talk of a world-man[38] as an ideal to be followed. And when the prevailingly atheist world has been permeated by the reality of God, atheism will no longer be so evident.

The spirituality of unity itself, which today is medicine for the times, when its purpose has been reached will be placed beside all the other various charisms that God has given to the Church throughout the centuries.

What remains, and what will always remain, is the gospel, which time cannot touch. "Heaven and earth will pass away, but my words will not pass away" (Mt 24:35). And this means all of Jesus' words.

I realize that we must, of course, adapt ourselves to the times we live in with all our strength, following all the particular inspirations that God gives us to bring God's kingdom ahead, which help it develop in ourselves and in those who are under our care. But we need to do everything with a sense that life is fleeting, knowing there is an eternal *Life* proclaimed by Jesus in his gospel.

We must give less importance in our hearts to all those ideas and methods that are useful, but not exclusively evangelical, and constantly renew our faith in the gospel, which will not pass away. This guarantees that a Movement like ours — open to *all*

---

38. This expression, which Chiara Lubich coined in her conversations with young people, is a plea to expand one's heart and mind as much as the forsaken Jesus did, in order to become people who are capable of effectively contributing to world unity. See Chiara Lubich, *Colloqui con i gen: Anni 1970–74* (Rome, 1999), pp. 73–83. *Ed.*

callings in the Church, each born of a word of God —
will continue.

We need always to return to our origins and
remember how God gave us an extremely precious
key to unlock the gospel. Of course, I am speaking of
our own story. It is tiny and brief, yet it remains a
necessary spark for us to ignite the gospel life
throughout the world.[39]

If we do this, the Work of Mary will truly continue
on earth as another Mary. It will be all gospel,
nothing but gospel, and because it is gospel, it will
never die.

---

39. This refers to the early history of the Focolare, when God inspired
Chiara Lubich and her original group of companions with ways to
develop the newborn spirituality of unity, which cuts to the heart of
the gospel and is based on Jesus' last prayer (Jn 17). See, for example,
Chiara Lubich, *Scritti Spirituali* 1 (Rome: Città Nuova, 1997), pp.
9–23. *Ed.*

3.
Mary, the Model of Perfection[1]

A New Way

Mary is the type and the form of the Church, and it is, therefore, evident that in such a sublime creature all Christians can find their own model. This was our experience as well, and perhaps in a special way: in fact, we discovered in Mary the model of our perfection.

Years ago, in 1961, the Lord led us to focus our attention on the following sentence from scripture: "For this is God's will, your sanctification" (1 Thes 4:3). As had happened before, we were struck by the fact that personal sanctification was not only for people called by God to a "state of perfection" but it was God's will for all Christians.

That same year, having read the spiritual writings of Teresa of Ávila, we realized that the members of the Movement, in their way to God (at least in the

---

1. A talk given at a meeting of bishops, friends of the Focolare Movement, 8 February 1988, in Castel Gandolfo (Rome). The author has revised it for the present publication.

initial part of their spiritual journey) passed through different moments, different stages, comparable to the ones described by the great reformer of Carmel, with specific characteristics, well-defined trials allowed by God, and typical effects after each trial had been overcome.

We noticed, for example, that people living in the midst of the world, perhaps caught up in sin, had begun to consider how life passes and that death will come; they had understood that it is important to do God's will, and that it is necessary to focus on the cross; they also felt a new desire for prayer, and for penance; they began to go to confession and receive the eucharist; women paid more attention to the way they dressed and men started cutting down on smoking, drinking, or superficial reading.

It became clear to us, therefore, that even though our way to God is lived in the midst of the world, while the way of Teresa of Avila was protected by monastic walls, growth and progress in the life of the soul had very similar characteristics. And we understood that if we were to continue on this path we would also come to experience the effects of the other stages that the saint of Avila speaks about, and we could consequently reach sanctity.

Such a realization filled us with gratitude, urging us to continue with increasing commitment on the road that we had taken.

After this discovery it became clear to us that our Movement had to be defined not only as making a contribution to the fulfillment of Jesus' last prayer,

"May they all be one" (Jn 17:21). Neither was it just a gospel-based movement with good effects in society. Nor was it only a movement with ecumenical aims, or had it come to life solely in order to give witness to the truth of Christ and his message to an unbelieving world. It was also a means to lead individuals to sanctity.

This, then, lead us to live our spirituality even more intensely.

It was a spirituality that focused above all on love. But since love is a source of light — as the scriptures say, "I will manifest myself to the one who loves me" (cf. Jn 14:21) — we soon had new insights into this way of sanctity.

One of our clearest insights at that time — which confirmed previous ones we have already spoken about — was this: God, while opening a way to sanctity, was also showing us a model we could imitate to reach it. This model was Mary.

The different moments in Mary's life as presented in the gospel, though extraordinary, appeared to us then as successive stages that we could refer to for light and encouragement in the different "ages" of our spiritual life.

This illumination was so strong that we called our way the "Way of Mary."

I will therefore give an outline of the stages of this way. But I must not fail to say that, as for every other way of perfection, they are always and only indications. The spiritual life is far more complex and varied, and is different for each individual person.

The Annunciation

The first event in Mary's life mentioned in the New Testament is the Annunciation (cf. Lk 1:25ff). Mary had been chosen by God from eternity, but something very special happened to her at the Annunciation. The angel appeared to her with a message from God, and Mary accepted it. Because of her yes, a new reality was immediately born within her: the incarnation of Jesus in her womb.

If we try to understand the lives of some saints, we can see that something analogous to what took place in Mary happens spiritually in them as well, when, for example, they come across a charism that God has given for the good of the Church.

We know the story of Saint Clare of Assisi, the most perfect disciple of Saint Francis.

It sometimes happens that, while visiting the Church of Saint Damian in Assisi, where she lived, the tour guide describes that sacred place by saying, "Here is where Christ was incarnated in the heart of Clare." And these are not just words; they reveal a profound truth.

Even though Clare of Assisi had, we may assume, lived in a state of grace, her meeting with Francis brought about something new in her. Francis was the personification of a word of God addressed to the world anew — the word "poverty." Meeting him caused Christ to develop and grow in Clare, to the extent that she became one of the greatest saints of the universal Church.

And is it not indeed the thought of popes, saints and Church Fathers, that the Word generates Christ in souls?[2]

Likewise, when at a certain point in our lives we come to know the charism of unity, through another person, a publication or a meeting, and we feel God's call to make it our own, if we say our yes, something similar to that which happened to Mary and the saints happens to us. Christ can truly begin to develop and grow spiritually in our hearts, as though by an actualization of our baptism.

The Visitation

The second episode in Mary's life was her visit to Elizabeth. Mary hastened to visit Elizabeth in order to help her. As she arrived, however, having found her relative open to the mysteries of God, Mary felt that she could share the great secret that she held in her heart, and she did so with the Magnificat: "My soul proclaims the greatness of the Lord; my spirit finds joy in God my savior. For he has looked upon his servant in her lowliness; all ages to come shall call me blessed" (Lk 1:46-48).

In this way Mary told Elizabeth about her extraordinary experience. We can grasp in the "Magnificat" that she gave expression to how Christ, who

---

2. Cf. Gregory the Great, *Hom. In Ev., cit.;* Paul VI, *Discorso,* in *Insegnamenti di Paolo VI,* Poliglotta Vaticana, V (1967), pp. 936, 938–39.

was already living in her, gave meaning to past centuries, to the present, and to centuries to come.

No sooner have those who know our Movement chosen God as the ideal of their lives than they feel that, in order to put this choice into practice, they have to begin to love. They approach those in need, as Mary did, and share in their sufferings and necessities.

What happens sometimes, though, is that because those who are approached are sensitive to charity, they realize that there is something in the heart of the persons helping them that makes them different. It is their availability to others and their joy. The people approached then ask to know the "secret" that makes them act as they do. The moment has arrived, for those who are part of the Movement, to tell of their spiritual experiences.

This is something new. Before coming to know God in a deeper way, they would not have been able to say anything very interesting about the spiritual aspect of their lives. Now instead, God who is living more intensely in their hearts enlightens them from within, almost explaining the plan he has for their lives. God sheds light on their past, on their present and towards the future of the divine adventure into which they have set out.

One of the characteristics of our Movement is precisely that of telling others the story of what meeting this ideal has done. In this way we share with each other the gifts we have received from God, for our mutual encouragement (cf. 1 Thes 5:11).

And this is a period of the spiritual life which, it seems to us, presents some analogy with Mary's meeting with Elizabeth.

By visiting Elizabeth, however, Mary did not only perform an act of charity, nor did she just sing the Magnificat. Christ's presence in her sanctified John the Baptist in the womb of his mother Elizabeth.

Keeping in mind the due proportions, something similar occurs when members of the Movement communicate something of Christ's presence in them by telling of their own spiritual experience with humility, objectivity and conviction. Often those who listen experience a special grace, an interior conversion. What is said is in fact more than just the story of an individual. In it one can see the blossoming of an age-old tree, which flowers in this season, giving witness to the vitality of the tree, which is the Church.

How often are individuals or groups of people who declare themselves to be atheists converted after simply listening to one of these experiences! Some of them, for example, exclaimed after listening to an experience, "Now we understand!" And to our question, "What did you understand?" they replied, "We have understood the revolution of Christ!" Through the little "revolution" that Christ had worked in one person, they understood Christianity.

The Birth of Jesus

The third event in Mary's life is the birth of Jesus (cf. Lk 2:7; Mt 1:25). Mary offers Jesus to the world.

When a person has been touched by the charism of unity, he or she starts to put it into practice by loving his or her neighbor. But further still, either because their neighbor learns to love in return, or because everyone who is part of our Movement generally strives to love, this love frequently becomes mutual.

There is a commitment, that is, to put into practice Jesus' command, "This is my commandment: love one another as I have loved you" (Jn 15:12).

The consequence of this is the fulfillment of Jesus' promise, "Where two or more are united in my name, there am I in the midst of them" (Mt 18:20). It is, in fact, mutual love that, according to the Church Fathers, allows us to reach unity in Jesus.[3] He establishes his spiritual presence in our midst when we love one another as he commands, when we are united in him.

This mutual love, therefore, which unites us in Jesus and brings about his presence among men and women, means, as Paul VI says, "generating Christ."[4] And this can come about in families, in factories, and in schools, places that become living cells of the

---

3. Cf. John Chrysostom, *In Inscript, Act. Apost.* 2, 4, in *Patrologia Greca* 51, 83; Teodoro Studita, *Epist II,* in *Patrologia,* in *Patrologia Greca* 99,1350; Origen, *Comm. In Matth. XIV,1,* in *Patrologia Greca,* 13, 1183–86.

4. Cf. *Discorso,* in *Insegnamenti di Paolo VI,* Poliglotta Vaticana, II (1964), pp. 1072–74.

mystical body, because Christ reigns among two or more: among husband and wife, among colleagues at work, and among friends.

Therefore, when — on the strength of the gift of unity — a member of the Movement becomes capable of generating the presence of Jesus in the midst with others, it can be said that he or she has reached the point of imitating Mary. For he or she gives Jesus to the world spiritually, as Mary did physically. Such person is therefore living the third stage of the "Way of Mary."

And this is a genuine stage, a true new moment of one's spiritual experience. We know the extraordinary effects produced by the presence of Jesus among people who are united in his name: a new joy, a new peace, love, patience, benevolence, goodness, faithfulness, meekness, self-control, that is, the fruits of the Spirit (cf. Gal 5:22), something similar perhaps, with due proportion, to the exultation Mary experienced when she brought Jesus into the world.

This is a stage in our spiritual journey that is hard to forget, at least in its first awakenings. Then we have to continue to live it each time God's will requests it. This brings about a birth and a rebirth of Jesus in our midst, which works for our sanctification and for the development of the Work of Mary that we are called to build, thus contributing to the renewal of the Church.

The Presentation of Jesus to the Temple

Continuing to follow Mary, we see her presenting her son at the temple and meeting the elderly Simeon. This is a joyous moment for the mother of Jesus, because that just and pious man confirms that this child is the Son of God, when he exclaims, "Now, Master, you can dismiss your servant in peace; you have fulfilled your word. For my eyes have witnessed your saving deed" (Lk 2:29-30).

However, it is also a moment of sorrow. Simeon, turning to Mary, adds "and a sword will pierce your own soul too" (Lk 2:35).

These were harsh words, which undoubtedly Mary would never be able to forget. They accompanied her all her life and prepared her for the deep sufferings that she would face.

Something somewhat similar happens also to all who live the spirituality of the Focolare.

In the beginning we are led on by enthusiasm, by the fascination of our newly discovered life, and by a special grace, which makes everything in this way of love appear easy and possible. But at a certain moment the Lord makes us understand, maybe through a talk, a writing, or a conversation, the indispensable condition for this ideal of unity to be authentic in our lives.

This is the moment when we hear of Jesus crucified and forsaken.[5] We understand that in order for us to

---

5. See pp. 77–81.

proceed along this way and be able to continue giving Jesus to the world, it is necessary for us to say yes to the cross, imitating what Mary must have said in the depth of her heart as she listened to Simeon. This is the moment when those who belong to the Movement are called to choose Jesus forsaken, the one who insures the unity of their souls with God, unity among themselves, and unity with the entire Work of Mary.

The Flight into Egypt

After the warning Simeon gave her, Mary immediately experienced a great suffering, that of the flight into Egypt (cf. Mt 2:13ff).

We can imagine how hard it must have been for her. She was experiencing persecution, a persecution stained by the blood of so many innocent children.

Something similar, in due proportion, happens to those who follow this "Way of Mary." The ideal of life that we offer to the world is also in opposition to it, because it is Jesus. And he is a sign of contradiction. It is not surprising, therefore, that when we start to live and spread this ideal, this may find some resistance. There may be some criticism, possibly from our own family, who may not understand the radical self-giving of someone called to follow Jesus, or from people who see in this renewed Christian life a kind of condemnation of their own mediocre way of living.

For those who suffer this kind of contention, this is the moment to take the necessary measures to save this "work" of God, in the vocations that have come into being and in the activities that have begun, just as Mary did with baby Jesus. We must remain closely united to those in whose care we are, follow their directives, and love and pray for those who are against us. The moment of the return from Egypt, that is, the day when these painful circumstances will finish, will come.

The Loss of Jesus in the Temple

When Jesus was about twelve years old, he remained with the teachers in the temple and his parents lost him for three days.

We can imagine Mary's bewilderment after having searched for and finally found Jesus, "Son, why have you done this to us? You see that your father and I have been searching for you in sorrow" (Lk 2:48).

In this new step in Mary's life, we see an analogy with something that typically occurs, at a certain spiritual age, to those who follow this path.

Having come to know and choose this new ideal of life and having lived up to the many graces the Lord has given till this point, they notice, perhaps even after years, a strong and insistent reappearance of temptations — temptations that through a special grace, which we believe are linked to this charism, seemed to have been completely overcome.

These temptations are generally against patience, charity, and chastity. At times they are so strong that they dim the light that had once fascinated us. Enthusiasm vanishes and progress is halted.

Such people suffer because of it and, turning to the Lord, they say in other words what Mary said, "Why have you gone so far from me? You have made your presence so deeply felt in my soul that I was beginning to believe that, with you, I could overcome every obstacle. Now here I am in the darkness of your absence."

And the Lord seems to say in reply, "Didn't you know that everything I gave you is mine and that you received it only and purely as a grace? Now they have been withdrawn and aridity and temptations have come upon you so that you might understand this clearly."

This process lays the foundation of humility that is necessary for Christ to live and to grow in each person.

The phenomenon that I am alluding to seems to have the typical features of one of the manifestations of what the mystics refer to as "the night of the senses."

For Mary, too, in a certain sense, the loss of young Jesus constituted a night of the senses. She could no longer see Jesus nor could she hear his voice. Her motherly love was deprived of his presence.

The Intimate Life of Nazareth

As far as we know, after this trial there was a long period in which Mary lived in the intimacy of the family with Jesus, and no one will ever know how divine, profound and full of spiritual consolations those years were. Their relationship, after that of the Persons of the Most Holy Trinity, was the most sublime and divine that could possibly be conceived.

It was the relationship between the Son of God and the one who was Immaculate.

In a similar way, those who accept with humility and overcome the previous stages then find themselves following their spiritual journey in a union with Jesus that is new and more profound. In it the Spirit gives, in a way that may even be constant, many of his gifts of confidence, peace, light, and love.

Saint Teresa says it is the kind of experience in which the soul touches the supernatural — a life of union with God that has no equivalent on earth and cannot be compared with any human love, no matter how great that love is.[6]

We can therefore say that Jesus' relationship with that soul is similar to what the gospel tells, "he subjected himself to them" (Lk 2:51). In a certain way, Jesus is at that person's disposal.

This period, though not lacking in crosses, can last a long time.

The Entry into Public Life

Then Jesus goes out into public life. Mary follows him in his mission, always with her heart and at times physically very closely.

For the persons of the Movement this period of Mary's life calls to mind that time in their spiritual life when, through the acquired habit of listening to

---

6. Teresa of Avila, *Relazioni spirituali*, 5, n. 8, in *Opere*, Rome, 1985, p. 472.

the voice of Jesus who speaks in their hearts and the voice of Jesus who lives among those who are united, they feel that voice as their own and they follow it. This voice grows so strong that it becomes absolutely the driving force for everything they do.

During his public life Jesus pronounced words of eternal life, he performed miracles, he trained disciples, he founded the Church.

Persons who reach this stage witness similar things done by Jesus in them personally, and by his presence among them. Jesus, in them, pronounces words that have the flavor of eternal life. Through them too, for example, Jesus works miracles of conversion; his presence in them also knows how to form disciples of this spirituality and thus spark new developments in the Work of Mary, for the advancement of the kingdom of God.

The Desolation

Then Mary reaches her hour of immolation. We have already mentioned it.[7]

Mary finds herself at the foot of the cross and Jesus turns to her and says: "Woman, behold your son!" and to John: "Behold your mother!" (Jn 19:26-27).

In that moment Mary, in an abyss of suffering whose depths we cannot measure, experiences the trial of losing the fruit of her womb, Jesus, the one who she could say was her purpose and work. It

---

7. See pp. 38–46.

seems Jesus is almost depriving Mary of her maternity toward him and transferring her motherhood to someone else, to John, in whom Jesus saw all of us. And Mary becomes mother to the whole of humanity, mother of the Church.

She pays for this with her own darkest desolation. She is alone, without Jesus. She is the Desolate. Here she lives the so-called "night of the spirit," because her heart echoes Jesus' cry on the cross, "My God, my God, why have you forsaken me?" (Mt 27:46).

Mariologists say that this was the moment the Virgin Mary reveals God's plan for her. His plan blossoms in full. Here she associates herself with Christ and fuses her passion with his, for the redemption of the human race.

In the Focolare, sufferings analogous to those of the Desolate are not lacking. In some of its members we can witness authentic symptoms of the "night of the spirit," when for example God permits someone to experience the terrible trial of feeling abandoned by him, or when faith, hope and charity are shaken. This can be seen to happen in persons who have spent their entire lives aiming at sanctity, and in the moments of their imminent passing to the next life they seem to climb the last steps of the "Way of Mary" with accelerated pace in their love for God. He prefers they experience purgatory in this life rather than in the next.

In those moments, along with Jesus forsaken, it is the Desolate that can be of light to their soul. It is from her that they learn to "stand upright" at the foot of the cross, while in deep agony of soul, completely accepting God's will just as Mary did (cf. Jn 19:25).

We often speak about the Desolate in the Focolare. And we try to imitate her also in other moments of the spiritual life, for instance when for some reason (sickness or changes of position) we have to abandon the work to which for years we have devoted all our efforts and our personal sacrifices, offering the blood of our souls for it. This is like losing "that Jesus" that we have in a certain way given our lives to.

Mary is also imitated when, through the most varied circumstances, persons find themselves without the spiritual help that seems so indispensable to them.

Or, moreover, when a person is sent alone to a country where the Focolare does not yet exist and must bring everything to life without the support and consolation of Jesus in the midst of brothers and sisters.

Mary in the Cenacle

And what happens after her desolation? Mary remains at the center of the Cenacle with all her maternal authority toward the Apostles, next to Peter, the one Jesus made their head.

Mary no longer "follows" Jesus: she is now in a certain way transformed into him. Before, since she was full of grace, she was already another Jesus, but now after the descent of the Holy Spirit, the words of Paul are true for her, and still more than they were for Paul: "It is no longer I who live, but Christ who lives in me" (Gal 2:20).

As another Christ, in her own way she too helps in working for the expansion of the Church.

This same goal, in due proportions, is what those who live the spirituality of unity strive for. This would be the stage mystics have called the transforming union, when — as Teresa of Avila says — Martha is joined to Mary: a particular work for the good of the Church is united to a particular contemplation.

In the saints, especially the great saints, it is not difficult to distinguish this moment in their ascent to God. After frightening dark nights, the Lord transforms them into himself, and so they reach the vocation of a Christian: *"dii estis"* — "you are gods" (Jn 10:34)[8] and do great things for the Spouse of Christ.

Assumption into Heaven

Finally, the moment of the Assumption arrives, when God calls Mary to heaven.

I read that Clare of Assisi before dying said these marvelous words, "I thank you, Lord, for having created me,"[9] meaning: by creating me you have acquired your own glory. Hers was a death of love.

If only heaven would wish something like this for us!

---

8. "This is why the Word became flesh and the Son of God became the Son of man: so that all people, united to the Word by receiving filial adoption, might become sons of God" (Iranaeus, *Adversus Haereses*, III, 19, 1, in *Patrologia Greca*, 7, 938).

9. See *Leggenda di Santa Chiara Vergine*, 46, in *Fonti Francescane*, Padova, 1980, p. 2432.

If we remain faithful, our own death too will not be simply a physical death, but a death of love. We too will rise up to meet our mother, our saint, our model, the one who on this earth was our head, our queen, and our mother.

And we will see the glory of Mary, queen of heaven and of earth. Above all, we will see her surrounded by those who loved her in a special way.

And we, each following the pattern of being a little Mary, will see ourselves surrounded by those who with our sacrifices, with our drops of blood joined to those of Mary and of Jesus, with our words, and with our prayers, we have helped to fulfill God's plan for them, helping them thus to reach paradise.

Imitating Mary

This is the "Way of Mary" as we have understood and experienced it in these sixty years of life. It is the way followed by those who have met the spirituality of the Work of Mary and made it their own.

Naturally, as I said at the beginning, it is a road that each person follows in a different way from anyone else, according to how each one lives up to what has been asked and to the graces that God freely bestows upon whom he wishes.

This diversity is characteristic of every spiritual path, and in a very particular way, this one, which is a path that is both individual and communitarian because of the constant presence of Jesus in the midst of those who come together in his name.

We also see that in this spirituality, besides following the traditional method, the Holy Spirit follows, as it were, a global method, where in every stage one can also experience a foretaste of the stages to come.

Mary therefore is the model of our sanctification. We rejoice and are grateful to see how her life sheds so much light on our own.

Paul says, "Be imitators of me, as I am of Christ" (1 Cor 11:1[10]). May we live our lives imitating Mary in such a way that each of us could say to the others: "Be imitators of me, as I am of Mary."

---

10. *"Imitatores mei estote, sicut et ego Christi,"* in the Vulgate.

4.

The Spiritual Influence of Mary on People Today[1]

A Spirituality That Is "All Hers"

I have to speak of Mary and her spiritual influence on contemporary society. This topic is especially dear to me in light of my work in the Church of spreading the charism of unity through the "Work of Mary" or "Focolare Movement."

Mary seems to be truly at work in this Movement, encouraging a communitarian, universal spirituality, one that is "all hers": the spirituality of unity, which teaches many men and women how to live as true Christians today. It is a way of living Christianity in our own time, confronting current problems and embracing the horizons opened up for us by the Second Vatican Council.

---

1. An address in the Basilica of Saint Mary Major, in Rome, on 30 November 1987 during the Marian Year.

God As Our Ideal

In this spirituality Mary is inviting people of our own day in particular to make an important decision; she is showing them the purpose of their lives, the ideal that should motivate them, and who they should have at the first place in their hearts.

As you know, today as always, people seek to give meaning to life, and they act with their specific goals in mind.

In Western society, for example, the ideal that inspires the masses is complete autonomy for the personality of the individual. Some would call this a desire for fullness of being, but it is in fact more about having than being. In reality, this way of looking at things becomes above all a pursuit of comfort and license in every area of life.

While there may be some positive aspects to these aspirations, like the promotion of human rights, of peace and security, one cannot deny that such a view of life is rather limited and full of risks.

People today, in fact, are overcoming barriers and prejudices in order to reach these goals of theirs, but in doing so they are also leaving behind values of the past that cannot be neglected or abandoned. As a consequence, they reduce to second place, and often overlook altogether, the transcendent dimension of life and the traditional rules of ethics. All these blameworthy behaviors do have an impact in some way or other on believers too, especially on the young.

Young people have a powerful desire to imitate "models," often superficial ones, which the world provides after its own materialistic and hedonistic fashion. Those things may provide a certain passing satisfaction and contentment, but they can also lead to grave consequences such as drugs, alcohol, crime and suicide, and this not just in rare cases.

Mary understands well the reality of our life on earth, as well as the life that opens to the future and lasts forever, and she speaks today to the human heart; she proposes that, in place of self-affirmation, personal autonomy, and well-being as goals of life (all futile ideals destined to pass away), we do as she has done and put God in the first place in our hearts.

Mary lived by God, by faith in God. For her, God was everything.

Moreover, God alone gives full meaning to life on this earth; God alone gives certainty to the life beyond, which is a reality that will last forever, even if people today do not often take it into account.

Yes, people today face a major conversion: away from themselves, where their lives are centered on their cravings and pleasures, and to God.

Faith in God-Love

How does Mary present God to people today?

She presents God in the fullness of the divine reality; she presents God as love. In fact, the true God, the God of Christianity, is love. Mary knows that by presenting God as God really is, we soon become aware that we are not alone in managing our own existence. We have with us one who loves us, who thinks of us, who is more of a Father than any earthly father. We come to understand that if such a Father as this was once able to send his own Son to earth to die for us and to save us from the snares of sin, we can be certain that he is able to intervene in every need, according to the word of Jesus, "Do not worry and say, 'What are we to eat?' or 'What are we to drink?' or 'What are we to wear?' . . . Your heavenly Father knows that you need them all" (Mt 6:31).

Believe in God-Love then. Live your life rooted in this faith. You can say of yourself the same thing that John the Evangelist wrote: "We have come to know and to believe in the love God has for us" (1 Jn 4:16). Yes, truly, if we believe, our life changes. That is everyone's experience.

Abandonment to the Plan of God

But it is not enough to stop at believing that God loves us. Mary teaches us that it is necessary to respond to God-Love by loving in return.

It is necessary to love God.

There is a passage in the gospel that shows clearly how we are to love God: "Not everyone who says to me, 'Lord, Lord,' will enter the kingdom of heaven, but only the one who does the will of my Father in heaven" (Mt 7:21).

Sometimes we think that to love God verbal expressions are enough, or that it is a matter of feelings. No. To love God means to do God's will. Not one's own will, but God's.

This means not to propose for our lives anything that is limited or inadequate, because it comes from us alone, but to abandon ourselves to carrying out the design that God in his love has planned for each of us. There is in fact for each of us a special design, marvelous and appealing, which brings happiness.

Today many people plan to sort themselves out financially and to have a good position in society.

Work is looked upon as a way of possessing tools of ever-increasing prosperity. Free time is directed toward collecting experiences, acquaintances, and pleasures. Travel, tourism, shows, and entertainment take priority as though they were everything. The pursuit of comfort leads to a smaller family, and to acquiring bit by bit a larger house, a second car, the latest in telecommunications, and so on.

These goals are completely secular and have lost every trace of Christianity. They give only passing earthly pleasure and certainly do not prepare for eternal life. Above all, these are goals that do not acknowledge what the human person could experience already in *this* life, if he or she were to live as a child of God.

If we decide in this earthly life not to do our own will but to do the will of God, who loves us as only God can, we prepare ourselves to turn this life into a wonderful, divine adventure. Those who do this, as

Mary and the saints did, know what extraordinary surprises await them.

When we do God's will, the Lord responds to our love with his own. If we give generously to our neighbors, he fills us with a superabundance of gifts; if we seek his kingdom, he gives us more than what we need as well; if we put him first in our hearts before family and possessions, he gives us a hundredfold. With the hundredfold he also gives eternal life.

We need to do God's will, then. And his will is made manifest to us, time after time, in different ways: sometimes in our own conscience or in the duties of our state in life; at other times in the commandments of God and the precepts of the Church. It is also revealed to us in daily events.

Love for Neighbor

There is a specific will of God, commanded by Jesus, that is especially emphasized by Mary.

It is love for neighbor. This is most important, because at the end of life we will be examined on it.

Jesus in fact will tell us: "For I was hungry and you gave me food, I was thirsty and you gave me drink, a stranger and you welcomed me, naked and you clothed me, ill and you cared for me, in prison and you visited me" (Mt 25:35-36).

We are to live this love for neighbor with everyone we encounter during the day, realizing that Jesus considers done to him what we do for that person. This includes our relatives whom we clothe, feed, console and counsel; it includes our colleagues at work, and members of the community whom we love by serving them in our offices, schools, government assemblies, and so on.

Love all, exclude no one. Love even your enemies. That is what it means to be a Christian.

Mutual Love

Christian love, however, is not one directional. It is not just directed toward others but it should also return to us. The pearl of the gospel is mutual love, love for one another, a love that is specifically Christian. "Love one another as I have loved you" (Jn 15:12). Mary, totally devoted to her son Jesus, reminds us that this commandment is especially dear to him, because he calls it his own commandment, a new commandment. It summarizes the entire gospel; it is Jesus' central teaching.

When Jesus came to earth, he did not come here out of nowhere, as the rest of us did, but rather he came from heaven.

As immigrants going off to a distant country adapt to their new environment but bring with them their own habits and customs, and often continue to use their own language, so Jesus adapted to life on earth. But, being God, he brought with him heaven's own lifestyle, that of the Trinity, which is love, mutual love.

This is what he wants for us, and Mary desires it for us as well. On the cross, Jesus made her our mother when he entrusted John to her, and she desires, as any good mother does, that people, her children, love one another. They are to love one another as Jesus loved them, by dying for them.

The first Christians understood Jesus' teaching of mutual love; they saw it as the focal point of the Good News and put it into practice with great zeal. In fact, when the pagans observed them they said, "See . . . how they love one another . . . they are ready to die for one another."[2]

It is necessary then that we too love one another, especially among Christians, putting this mutual love at the basis of everything we do, as scripture dictates. Does not Jesus admonish us that, when we are offering our gift at the altar and there remember that our brother or sister has something against us, that it is better not to make the offering but to go first and be reconciled? That is how important fraternal love is for him. It is almost the whole of Christianity. If we love one another, every thing we do, no matter how small and humble, takes on value.

Mutual love will, moreover, be a fountain of renewed joy in our lives; it will be a source of light and of peace, because love draws the fruits of the Spirit to itself.

The Presence of Jesus in Our Midst

When we love one another as Jesus has loved us, among other things we experience a supernatural

---

2. Tertullian, *Apologetica*, 145.

phenomenon in our lives. Jesus makes himself spiritually present among us, for he said, "For where two or three are gathered together in my name, there am I in the midst of them" (Mt 18:20).

Mary very much loves this presence of Jesus among her children. She who physically gave Jesus to the world wants nothing more than to see him living spiritually in the world today among Christians.

It is necessary, therefore, to strive for mutual love with all our heart.

If we love one another, we will be able to radiate Christianity fully and effectively in the midst of the secularized society in which we live, because people today will believe precisely because of our mutual love. Jesus said, "So that they may all be one [in love] that the world may believe" (cf. Jn 17:21). This is what the first Christians experienced.

Such was the divine power that emanated from this way of living Christianity that in a short time Christians were spread throughout the world and were present practically in every part of the known world. Tertullian tells us, "We began yesterday: but we have already encompassed the whole world."[3]

What an ideal for us as well!

A New Explanation of Suffering

To choose God-Love as the ideal of one's life, to do his will by responding to it with one's love, above all to love one's neighbor and love one another — these

---

3. Tertullian, *ibid.*, 139.

are the initial teachings Mary offers us through the charism of unity.

But this is not all. Mary also gives people today a new explanation of suffering.

She fully confronts this problem facing people in every age and challenging every person, a problem that often seems to have no answer.

What meaning does suffering have for Mary? What is the best way to face it?

Except for a small number of believers who are practicing their faith and, especially, for an elite actually involved in living a Christian life, most people today view suffering with fear, because it is not understood and hence not even thought about. Shows, television, and advertising all try to present an atmosphere of security and well-being. Above all, any thought of death is excluded, as if it did not exist, and the attention is carefully turned to things that one can enjoy in *this* world. Whatever brings suffering is viewed simply as bad luck.

But the mystery of suffering has a different meaning.

The one who has explained it by word and by example is Jesus.

He suffered and died. Of course this was all brought about by evil on the part of those who condemned, scourged, and crucified him. But he always saw a deeper motivation behind his suffering and death. He suffered and died for us, because we had separated ourselves from God through sin, in order to reunite us to God and to one another.

From the moment that Jesus was on the cross, every one of our sufferings has taken on a similar meaning to his.

Of course we suffer from adverse causes like accidents, sickness or misfortunes. But God, who is love for us as he was for Jesus, reveals another meaning to suffering. Through it we contribute to our salvation and sanctification, and to that of our brothers and sisters. In this way, like Jesus, we and our brothers and sisters will come to see the resurrection, which is the beginning of full and unending life.

The saints understood and understand this new way of viewing suffering. In every trial and every cross they looked beyond the external, material, and temporal aspect and are able to perceive the hand of God allowing it, so that through Christ it may be for their spiritual good and for that of others.

Thus, in looking upon Christ crucified they discover the value of suffering. They are able to identify with him and reach union with God.

For example, Clare of Assisi, after standing for a long time before the crucifix at San Damiano, returned to her companions with her face aglow, showing her growing unity with the Lord.

And Bonaventure, having passed spiritually through the wounds of Jesus, was engulfed in the flames of the furnace of divine love which is his heart.

And Catherine of Siena used the two images of "blood and fire" to teach the importance of accepting suffering so as to burn with the love of God.

Today, in the experience of the Focolare Movement, Our Lady points to a particular suffering of

Jesus, his greatest suffering, when he cried out, "My God, my God, why have you forsaken me?" (Mt 27:46).

In that terrible moment, the Son of God had the impression that the Father, who was one with him, had abandoned him. The torment he experienced within was so deep that it defies imagination. He experienced in his divine heart the separation from God that humankind suffers by sin with all its consequences. His spirit was plunged into the deepest darkness, the most dreadful doubt, with a total loss of peace; he felt the entire weight of our sins which he had taken upon himself. But in spite of everything he again placed all his trust in the Father. "Father," he said, "into your hands I commend my spirit" (Lk 23:46).

By focusing our attention on Jesus crucified and forsaken, Mary wants to help us find the strength to overcome every obstacle.

If we too suffer from some loss of peace, tranquility, or security, we should remember the suffering of Jesus. If we find dryness, darkness and confusion within, or if we are gripped by doubt or the weight of our sins, we should think of him. We should go into the depths of our hearts and tell him that we want to do as he did: accept suffering and give him our yes. If we do so and continue to live our life as Christians, we will experience among other things that suffering, especially spiritual suffering, when we embrace it, is almost miraculously transformed by a divine alchemy into love. Suffering, if well endured, will increase our union with God and help others to find such union and increase it as well.

Universal Brotherhood

Finally, through the charism of unity, Mary extends a further invitation to people today. She directs them to a universal brotherhood, the unity of the human family.

Even though our planet is beset with many tensions, Our Lady leads us in various ways to unity, and she desires this for all. She wants families united, different generations united; she asks for unity among different ethnic groups, races and peoples; unity among Christians and unity, as far as it is possible, with the faithful of other religions and even with those who have no specific religious affiliation but seek the welfare of humankind. She reaches out to everyone, and she desires universal brotherhood.

With Mary, the First Layperson in the Church

So these are some of the things that Mary has shown us through an ecclesial Movement in the Church.

If we were to put into practice with all our energy just one of her requests, we would experience something truly new in our lives as Christians.

Millions all over the world already, with great spiritual joy, follow these things suggested by Mary, which are actually very universal, and find the solution to many personal, family and social problems. They are transformed into authentic apostles of a new civilization of love.

May Mary, who made God the ideal of her life, help us make him our ideal as well.

May Mary, who embraced the will of God in the incarnation and in her whole life, help us to fulfill his will to perfection.

May she, who loved her neighbor as demonstrated in her visit to Elizabeth and at the wedding at Cana, fill our hearts with this same love.

May Mary, who lived mutual love fully in the family at Nazareth, help us to practice it as well.

May Mary, who was able to offer all her suffering at the foot of the cross, strengthen our hearts when we are besieged by suffering.

May Mary, who is the universal mother, open our hearts to all humankind.

With her, the first layperson in the Church, and through her spirituality, also we, lay people, can be capable undertaking the task to which the Church calls us today: working for our sanctification, which is the vocation of all Christians; contributing to the renewal of the Church and spreading its message; transforming in a Christian way the world in which are immersed. And may all this be to the glory of God and his mother.

5.

Mary, Mother of Unity[1]

1. A few of Chiara's writings in this chapter have already been published in English, and some are cited in the second chapter of the present book. Nonetheless, it is useful to gather together the complete versions of these texts to continue and expand upon the thoughts of the preceding pages. *Ed.*

As a Heavenly Plane Sloping

Mary is not easily understood even though she is greatly loved. In a heart that is far from God, one is more likely to find devotion to her than to Jesus.

She is universally loved.

And the reason is this: it is Mary's nature to be *Mother*.

Mothers, in general, are not "understood," especially by younger children; they are "loved." And not infrequently, indeed often, one hears that an eighty-year-old man dies saying as his last word: "mother."

A mother is more the object of the heart's intuition than of the mind's speculation. She is more poetry than philosophy, because she is too real and profound, close to the human heart.

So it is with Mary, the Mother of mothers, who the sum of all the affection, goodness, and mercy of all the mothers in the world cannot manage to equal.

Jesus, in a certain sense, *confronts* us more: his divine and splendid works are too different from ours to be confused with them. Indeed they are a sign of contradiction.

Mary is peaceful like nature, pure, serene, clear, temperate, beautiful — that nature which is distant from the world, in the mountains, in the open countryside, by the sea, in the blue sky or the starry heavens. She is strong, vigorous, harmonious, consistent, unyielding, rich in hope, for in nature it is life that springs up perennially generous, adorned with the fragrant beauty of flowers, kind in the abundance of its fruits.

Mary is too simple and too close to us to be "contemplated."

She is "sung" by hearts that are pure and in love, who express like this what is best in them. She brings the divine to earth as gently as a heavenly plane sloping from the dizzy heights of heaven to the infinite smallness of creatures. She is the Mother of all and of each human being, who alone knows how to burble and smile at her child in such a way that, even though it is small, each knows how to enjoy her caress and respond with its love to *that* love.

Mary is not understood because she is too close to us. She, who was destined from eternity to bring graces, the divine jewels of her Son, to humanity, is there, near to us, and waits, always hoping for us to notice her gaze and accept her gifts.

If any are fortunate enough to understand her, she carries them off to her kingdom of peace, where Jesus is King, and the Holy Spirit is the life-breath of that heaven.

There, purified of our dross and illuminated in our darkness, we will contemplate her and enjoy her, an added paradise, a paradise apart.

Here, let us be found worthy of being called along "her way" to avoid staying always immature in spirit, with a love that does not go beyond supplication, petition, request and self-interest, but knowing her a little, may we glorify her.[2]

---

2. 1958.

Mary, Flower of Humanity

When we look at nature, it seems that Jesus gives it his new commandment too.

I observed two plants and I thought about pollination. Before this happens the plants grow upward, as if they were loving God with all their being. Then they unite, almost as if they were loving one another as the Persons of the Trinity love one another. From two they become one. They love one another to the point of abandonment, to the point of losing their personalities, so to speak, like Jesus in his forsakenness.

Then, from the flower that blossoms, a fruit is born and life, therefore, continues. It is like God's eternal Life which is imprinted in nature.

The Old and the New Testaments form a single tree.

Its flowering happened in the fullness of time, and its only flower was Mary.

The fruit which followed was Jesus.

The tree of humanity was also created in the image of God.

When, in the fullness of time, it blossomed, unity was made between heaven and earth, and the Holy Spirit espoused Mary.

Therefore, there is one flower: Mary. And there is one fruit: Jesus. And Mary, though alone, is nevertheless the synthesis of the entire creation in the culminating moment of its beauty when it presents itself as spouse to its Creator.

Jesus, instead, is creation and the uncreated made one: the Marriage consummated. And he contains Mary within himself just as the fruit contains the flower. Once the flower has served its purpose, it falls and the fruit matures.

Even so, if there had never been a flower, then neither would the fruit have ripened.

Just as Mary is daughter of her Son, similarly, the flower is child of the fruit which is its child.

Yet the time span between the flower and the fruit is so short that it is almost annulled, since fruit is the result of the flower.

Whereas the flower, following a long duration, is born by the tree, generated by the seed contained within the fruit.

Likewise, Mary is the flower blossoming on the tree of humanity, born of God who created the first seed in Adam. She is daughter of God her Son.

As I watched a small geranium breaking into a flower of red, I wondered to myself and asked it: "Why are you flowering in red? Why do you change from green to red?" It seemed such a strange thing to me!

Today I understood that all of humanity flowers in Mary. Mary is the flower of humanity. She, the Unstained, is the flower of the stained.

Sinful humanity flowered in Mary, the All Beautiful!

And just as the red flower is grateful to the small green plant, with its dirt-covered roots, which made her flower; so too is Mary grateful to sinners like us who constrained God into thinking of Mary.

We owe our salvation to her; she owes us her existence.

How beautiful Mary is! She is creation in flower, creation turned beautiful. Mary is all of creation in flower, like the foliage covering the tree. From his heavenly heights, God fell in love with this flower of flowers. He pollinated her with the Holy Spirit, and Mary gives to heaven and earth the fruit of fruits: Jesus.

In order to descend, the Lord God of heaven had to find Mary. He could not descend into sin, and, therefore, he "invented" Mary, who, gathering in herself all of the beauty of creation, "tricked" God and drew him to earth.

Yet she is the flower of humanity, and calling God to herself, she calls him *for* humanity, because she is grateful to humanity for having given her life.[3]

---

3. 9 July 1950.

Mother of God

Then I looked above me, at a beautiful statue of the Madonna, and I understood how she was entirely *Word of God*. I saw her beautiful beyond all telling: completely clothed with the Word of God who is the Beauty of the Father, she, secret guardian of the *Spirit within her*.

And as soon as I loved her, she loved me, and showed me with heavenly clarity her full beauty: *Mother of God!*

Outside, the sky was blue as never before. . . . Then I understood: the sky contains the sun! Mary contains God! God loved her so much that he made her his mother, and his Love made himself small in front of her![4]

---

4. 19 July 1949.

Perfect, But Perfectible

Mary was perfect, though always perfectible because the Holy Spirit was growing in her.

Jesus could not do anything but the Father's will. He could not do his mother's will unless hers was the identical will of the Father.

When Mary said something to Jesus, she said it the way she felt it, through the Holy Spirit that was in her.

But Jesus — being perfect while not perfectible — had Mary renounce her own will . . . strengthening her capacity to acquire ever more the Holy Spirit. And so it seemed he treated her harshly, because he loved her. . . .

She, obedient, submitted herself to her Son's will, which enlarged her heart, giving her a greater love, and with this love of hers (become Jesus) she was the Light of Jesus in such a way that he did her will which became his will, that is, the Father's will. In this way Jesus continually raised Mary to the "greatness" of God the Father. . . . Perhaps only now we can understand Jesus' words, "Woman, how does this concern of yours involve me?" (Jn 2:4), as though to say: "Remember that there is an abyss between you and me. . . : therefore! Enter in me and do with me the will of the Father."[5]

---

5. July 28, 1949.

Invincible

The heavenly Mother was infinitely empty, and so, invincible. Who could find her in order to strike her if she was not there?[6]

---

6. 26 July 1949.

Mother of All

When Jesus said: "Woman, behold your Son" (Jn 19:26), Mary was no longer his Mother. It is the moment that Mary gives back to God the divine maternity that he shared with her.

It is a different *fiat* from the first: with the first she renounced her virginity, apparently; with the second she renounces her Motherhood — also apparently. Only in this way could Mary become mother of all. Mary acquires the *divine* maternity of infinite souls through renouncing the divine maternity of her First Son. And even this accords with God's plans. She gives one and receives a hundredfold.[7]

---

7. 2 October 1949.

The Desolate

I have only one mother on earth:
Mary Desolate.
I have no mother but her.
In her is the whole Church for eternity,
and the whole Work of Mary in unity.
In her design is mine.
I will go through the world reliving her.
Every separation will be mine.
Every detachment from the good I have done
will contribute to building up Mary.
In her "staying" (at the foot of the cross),
my "staying."
In her "staying," my "going."
Hortus conclusus, enclosed garden,
Sealed fountain (cf. Song 4:12);
I will cultivate her most loved virtues,
so that on the silent nothingness of myself
her wisdom may shine.
That many, all her chosen children,
the most needful of her mercy,
may always find her maternal presence
in another little Mary.[8]

---

8. 20 August 1962.

Gate of Heaven

The Desolate has her own Wound too. It is the Wound placed in her heart by the forsakenness of Jesus: "Woman, behold your Son!" (Jn 19:26)... (the silence of the One replaced by John is the summit of her suffering, comparable to God's silence in Jesus' forsakenness). . . .   Into that Wound entered John and with him the whole of the human race. The children of humanity entered back into the most pure womb of Mary, from which came forth the Son of God, in order to be divinized . . . in Mary. She is the Gate of Heaven. We cannot be Christian if we are not Marian. We cannot be divine if we are not immaculate. We cannot go to Jesus except through Mary. We cannot possess the Forsaken One if not through the one who was Desolate.[9]

---

9. 28 September 1949.

Word of God

To be Mary we must be Jesus Forsaken[10] or also Mary Desolate: offering ourselves to suffer the absence of the Son, rejoicing at being without peace, joy, health . . . all that she is: to feel ourselves to be her in her desolation. . . .

". . . because you are desolate,"[11] and therefore be *only* Word of God. To guard within ourselves only the Word of God.[12]

The Word was always in her (Mary). That is how our souls should be: living always with the Word: focused totally and focused only on the Word. And the secret to doing that: to live as if everything depends on my own love: "*pro eis sanctifico me ipsum*" — "For their sakes I sanctify myself" (Jn 17:19)[13]

---

10. See pp. 77–81.
11. See p. 19.
12. 27 July 1949.
13. 26 July 1949.

Jesus' Masterpiece

Jesus' masterpiece is Mary, his greatest work: she, the Father's perfect daughter, who corresponded most perfectly to grace, who took full advantage of the redemption.[14]

---

14. 5 July 1950.

Queen of the Apostles

Our Mother is so beautiful in her continuous recollection as shown us by the gospel: "But Mary kept all these things, pondering them in her heart" (Lk 2:19).

That full silence fascinates the soul who loves.

How can I live like Mary in her mystical silence when my vocation is to speak in order to evangelize, always exposed in every kind of place, rich and poor, from cellars to government offices, from streets to monasteries and convents?

Our Mother also spoke. *She said Jesus. She gave Jesus.* There has never been a greater apostle in the world. No one ever spoke such words as she, who gave and said the *Word*.

Our Mother is truly and deservedly called Queen of the Apostles.

And she kept silent. She kept silent because the two could not speak at once. The word must always rest against a silence, like a painting against a background.

She kept silent because she was a creature. For nothingness does not speak. But upon that nothingness Jesus spoke and said: himself. God, Creator and All, spoke upon the nothingness of the creature.

How then can I live Mary, how can my life be perfumed by her beauty?

By silencing the creature in me, and upon this silence letting the Spirit of the Lord speak.

In this way I live Mary and I live Jesus. I live Jesus upon Mary. I live Mary by living Jesus. I live Jesus by living Mary.[15]

---

15. Summer 1950.

The *Magna Carta*

The *magna carta* of Christian social doctrine begins with the words of Mary's song: "He has deposed the mighty from their thrones and raised the lowly to high places. The hungry he has given every good thing, while the rich he has sent empty away" (Lk 1:52-53).

The gospel contains the greatest and most sweeping revolution. And perhaps it is part of God's plans that in this age, deeply concerned as it is with seeking solutions to social problems, it would be Mary to give us Christians a hand to build, consolidate, raise up and show the world a new society that strongly echoes the Magnificat.[16]

---

16. April 1950.

Queen of the World[17]

If one day all people, not as individuals, but as peoples, if one day all peoples would learn to put themselves aside, to put aside the ideas they have about their own countries, their kingdoms, and offer them as incense to the Lord, the king of a kingdom that is not of this world, the guide of history, and if all would do this as the expression of the mutual love between states that God asks for, just as he asks for mutual love among individuals, that day would be the beginning of a new era. For on that day, just as Jesus is present among two who love each other in Christ, Jesus will be alive and present among peoples, given finally his true place as the one king, not only of individual hearts but of nations: he will be Christ the King.

Christian peoples, or their representatives, must learn how to sacrifice their "collective" egos. This is the price. Nothing less is asked of each of us in order for our souls to be consumed in unity. Now is the time for every people to go beyond its own borders, to look farther. Now is the time to love the other coun-

---

17. A talk given at Fiera di Primiero (Italy) on 22 August 1959, the feast of Mary Queen of the World, when the participants of the Focolare summer gathering, the Mariapolis, wished solemnly to consecrate themselves and their nations to Mary.

tries as our own, to acquire a new purity of vision. To be Christians it is not enough to be detached from ourselves. The times we live in demand from the followers of Christ something more: the awareness of Christianity's social dimension, which not only builds up one's own land according to the law of Christ but assists in the building up of all other lands as well, through the universal action of the Church, and through the supernatural vision given to us by God the Father, who sees things quite differently from the way we do. We need to live the Mystical Body of Christ in such an excellent way as to translate it into the mystical body of society.

History speaks almost exclusively of wars, and as children in school we have learned almost that wars are good and holy, almost the safeguard of our homelands. This may be so and sometimes it was so.

But if we hear echoing in our souls the appeals of the popes, like Pope Pius XII, we will recognize how they feared war, for the sake of humanity, and how they reached out to government leaders, whether they were asked to or not. They strove to appease anger and self-interest in order to avoid the disaster of war that destroys everything, while with peace everything is gained.

For history is a series of fratricidal conflicts among brother nations, whose lands were given them by the one Master of the world, to live on and to cultivate.

He blesses peace because he is peace in himself. We see how one by one the Lord is conquering the hearts of his children of all nations and languages, transforming them into children of love, joy, peace, ardor, and strength. And we hope that the Lord may have mercy on this divided and confused world, on peoples closed within their shells contemplating their own beauty — the only beauty that exists for them (though it is both limiting and unsatisfying). They strain to hold onto their treasures against all odds, the very treasures that could help other peoples who are dying of hunger. May the Lord cause all barriers to fall, and allow love to run uninterrupted through all lands, flooding them with spiritual and material goods.

Let's hope that the Lord brings about a new order in the world. He is the only one who can make humanity a family and cultivate the unique characteristics of each people so that the splendor of each, placed at the service of others, may shine with the one light of life. This light of life in making beautiful each earthly country will make it the antechamber of the eternal.

It may seem like a dream. But (apart from the fact that if the relationship among Christians is one of mutual love, then the relationship among Christian peoples cannot but be one of mutual love, because of the gospel logic which does not change) there exists a bond that even now powerfully unites peoples to one another. It has already been proclaimed by the voice of the people, by every people, in the voice of the people that is often the voice of God. This bond hidden and cherished in the heart of every nation is Mary.

Who can take away from the Brazilians the idea that Mary is the Queen of their land?

And who can tell the Portuguese that Mary is not "Our Lady of Fatima"?

Who does not acknowledge to the French the beautiful Lady of Lourdes?

And to the Polish the Madonna of Czestochowa?

To the English, that their land is "Mary's Dowry"?

Who can deny that Mary is the "Châtelaine of Italy"?

How often in history have peoples taken refuge at their Marian grottos, basilicas, or shrines, as though seeking protection under Mary's mantle when their brothers of other nations attacked them. All Christian peoples have proclaimed her Queen, for themselves and for their children.

But one thing is missing, and this is something Mary cannot do. We have to help her: what is missing is our collaboration so that Catholic peoples, united as brothers and sisters, go to her and recognize her as both Mother and Queen. We can crown her as such only if, through our conversion, through our prayers, and through our actions, we take away the veil that still covers her crown, even though the crown was given to her by the Pope long ago when he proclaimed her Queen of the world and of the universe. We must each place at her feet the piece of the world that is in our hands.

If today non-Christian laws have almost made some of the boundaries disappear among peoples who are yet still very Christian, perhaps God is permitting this so that the progress of Mary in the world, which must come, be less obstructed. In this way everything can become her "footstool" (cf. Mt

5:35), footstool of she who is the greatest queen known to heaven and earth: Queen of all Humanity, Queen of Saints, Queen of Angels – all because on earth she knew how to sacrifice herself totally, becoming the servant of the Lord, and is thus able to teach her children the way of unity, of the universal embrace of all human beings, so that everything may be "on earth as it is in heaven."

I Want to See Her Again in You

I went into church one day,
and with my heart full of trust, I asked:
"Why did you wish to remain on earth,
in the most sweet Eucharist,
and you have not found
— you who are God —
also a way to bring and to leave here
Mary, the mother of all of us who journey?"
In the silence, he seemed to reply:
"I have not left her
because I want to see her again in you.
Even if you are not immaculate,
my love will virginize you,
and you, all of you,
will open your arms and hearts
as mothers of humanity,
which, as in times past, thirsts for God
and for his mother.
It is you who now
must soothe pains, soothe wounds,
dry tears.
Sing her litanies
and strive to mirror yourself in them.[18]

_____

18. December 1957.